HEMI
MUSCLE CARS

Robert Genat

MBI Publishing Company

For my good friend Joe Veraldi.

Acknowledgments

Thanks to the following Hemi car owners for their patience and understanding during the photographic process. Kenn Funk, Gil Funk, Harold Sullivan, Mick Weise, Kirk Richardson, Gil "Hemi Gil" Garcia, Akbar Aly, Emilio "Hemi Jac" Parra, Greg Joseph, Fred DeWitte, Jr., Mel Wojtynek, Anatol and Susan Vasiliev, Ivan Daigle, Bill Wages, Bob Karakashian, John Bailey, Bob McLeod, and Nick Bigioni.

Thanks to the following for their many and varied contributions. Charlie DiBari, Norm "Mr. Norm" Kraus, Dick Landy, Robert Landy, Robert Tornio, Larry Weiner, Mark Farrin, Becky Ferrell, Bob Mosher, Bob LaBonte, Bob Riggle, Dan Jensen, Jerry Pitt, Richard Jankowski, and Gary Jankowski. A special thanks to Art Ponder of Chrysler Historic and Dale Amy for sharing his excellent photography.

First published in 1999 by MBI Publishing Company, 729 Prospect Avenue, PO Box 1, Osceola, WI 54020-0001 USA

MBI Publishing Company books are also available at discounts in bulk quantity for industrial or sales-promotional use. For details write to Special Sales Manager at Motorbooks International Wholesalers & Distributors, 729 Prospect Avenue, Osceola, WI 54020-0001 USA.

Library of Congress Cataloging-in-Publication Data
Genat, Robert.
    Hemi muscle cars/Robert Genat.
      p. cm.––(Enthusiast color series)
    Includes index.
    ISBN 0-7603-0635-4
    1. Chrysler automobile––History. 2. Muscle cars––History.
3. Chrysler automobile––Motors––History. I. Title. II. Series.
TL215.C55G45   1999
629.222'2––dc21   99-14540

On the front cover: The 1971 'Cuda carries the legendary 426 Hemi powerplant that was rated at 425 horsepower, but actual output was closer to 500. Ford and GM attempted to topple the dominance of the Hemi, but this engine took the Charger, Barracuda, Road Runner, Plymouth Superbird, and other Chrysler models to the top of the sport. In the final analysis, Hemi-powered cars are the ultimate definition of the high-performance musclecar.

On the frontispiece: These "hockey stick" stripes appear on the rear quarter panels of this 1970 'Cuda and don't leave anything to the imagination. In no uncertain terms, they shout to the world that the 'Cuda is powered by Chrysler's most formidable engine—the Hemi. The relatively compact E-bodied 'Cuda, created to challenge the Mustang and Camaro, is the fastest of the Hemi-powered street cars.

On the title page: Even under hard acceleration, your eye can catch the "Hemi" on this 1970 'Cuda's hockey stick stripe.

On the back cover: There is no mistaking the one-of-a-kind profile of the 1970 Plymouth Superbird. With its elongated front fascia and huge rear wing, it dominated NASCAR stock car racing during the 1970 season. It was so dominant that it was banned the following year. The street version never caught the public's attention and sales stagnated. Today, it is one of the rarest and most sought after Hemi musclecars ever built.

Edited by Paul Johnson

Printed in Hong Kong

Contents

Introduction

Hemi! One word says it all. At a car show or drag race, a Hemi-powered car stops people in their tracks. It's the one musclecar that knows no manufacturer-biased boundaries. Although many of the most die-hard Ford and GM enthusiasts won't admit it, they hold the Hemi engine and Hemi-powered musclecars in high esteem.

By the late 1960s, the Hemi upped the performance ante so high that the others couldn't even compete. Soon, it was Hemi versus Hemi, with all the others racing each other at the back of the pack. In NASCAR racing, the Hemi's performance tipped the scale so far that it was banned. It was so powerful, so potent a machine, and so far above the competition that the playing field had to be leveled.

In pure stock form, the Hemi was more than the equal of the other engines. When modified, it was unbeatable. The Hemi engine had more potential for pure horsepower than any other musclecar engine. In addition, these monster engines were installed in some of the finest-looking cars Chrysler ever offered.

During the few years that the Hemi was available, approximately 11,000 were delivered. In sheer numbers, the Hemi production was a mere grain of sand in the desert of automotive-production history. But to automotive enthusiasts and historians, the era of the Hemi was monumental. Every gearhead remembers the first Hemi car he

saw. It may have been at a drive-in, at the drag strip, or on a smooth strip of onyxlike asphalt. Those who have competed against a Hemi on the street or the track know what it's like because they are so hard to beat.

For the 1966 model year, Chrysler faced a costly dilemma. In order to race its Hemi engine in NASCAR, Chrysler had to build assembly-line versions. The company knew that its image on the track heavily contributed to showroom sales, so it created street going Hemis for 1966. Unfortunately, Chrysler didn't realize any profits from those models. Fitting the large Hemi into the engine bay of the Dodge Coronet and the Plymouth Belvedere and Satellite models was relatively easy. Designers beefed up the drive train and suspension to complement the Hemi's immense horsepower potential.

To make the Hemi streetable, Chrysler's engineers had to detune the powerful race engine. The aluminum heads were replaced with cast-iron versions. The compression was dropped by 2 1/4 to 10.25:1, so it could run on premium pump gas. The cross-ram intake was replaced with an aluminum manifold fitted with two Carter AFBs in tandem. For cold weather operation, a choke was provided along with manifold heat. Cast-iron exhaust manifolds replaced the tubular exhaust headers. The Hemi's horsepower rating was listed as 425 at 5,000 rpm, but Chrysler engineer Tom Hoover once stated that the street Hemi actually produced 500 horsepower at 6,000 rpm, a number Chrysler was hesitant to advertise.

The Hemi cars featured in this book cover only the years 1964 through 1971. These cars were either built at a Chrysler assembly plant or by a subsidiary under contract to Chrysler. In NASCAR racing, the race teams obtained engines and chassis through special racing channels (i.e., the factory race shops), not from the dealership's showroom floor. The Daytona Chargers and Super Birds, spawned by NASCAR competition and delivered to the general public, are prominently featured.

This book covers a wide range of Hemi-powered cars; some have been restored to perfection and others are original low-mileage survivors. A few are never driven and many others are cruised to car shows and occasionally used for daily errands. (Following one photo session, the owner was hungry and took his rare Hemi car through a local fast food drive-through.) Three of the Hemi cars in this book were raced extensively, have since been restored to their factory-fresh glory, and are now driven on the street. One of the race cars is still actively raced.

The street Hemi engine was first released in 1966 to satisfy NASCAR's rules requiring that the engine be production based. In this same basic form, the street Hemi was installed in 11,000 Dodges and Plymouths through the 1971 model year. Chrysler Historical

1

The Fabulous Chrysler B-Bodies

Coronet, Belvedere, GTX, RT, Road Runner, and Super Bee

In 1966, Chrysler's mid-size cars were not as flashy as their contemporaries from General Motors and Ford. General Motors' and Ford's musclecars were given special trim and badges announcing their high-performance heritage to the world. On the street, it was easy to spot a Pontiac GTO, a Chevy 396SS, or a Ford Fairlane GT. Chrysler took a much more low-key approach to its musclecars, especially the Hemi. It would have been difficult at night on Woodward Avenue to read the small HEMI badging on the side of a 1966 Belvedere or Coronet. But as soon as the light turned green, the Hemi would be gone like a shot.

All 1966 B-bodies, from both Dodge and Plymouth, were built on the previous year's platforms. The Dodge Coronet was offered in four trim levels:

The 1969 Road Runner continued the momentum of the 1968 model. In the Road Runner, the public was offered a highly identifiable musclecar at a low price. In addition, engine options and creature comforts were available at an extra cost.

9

the base Coronet, the Coronet Deluxe, and the Coronet 440 and 500. The 440 and 500 were only used to distinguish the differences in the series of cars and had nothing to do with engine size. The 1966 Coronet featured a finely sculpted body in both sedan and hardtop versions. Car buyers were accustomed to seeing something new each year, and the new Coronet didn't disappoint its fans. The big news was the addition of the powerful 426-ci street Hemi engine to the option list. Dodge now

had a full-fledged musclecar. Unfortunately, the new Coronet didn't have the visual appeal to match its horsepower, but that would soon change. Hemi sales were brisk, with over 740 Coronet customers checking the box on the order sheet for the elephant engine.

Like the Dodge Coronet, the 1966 Plymouth Belvedere and Satellite both had gracefully contoured sides. At 116 inches, the Plymouth rode on a wheelbase one inch shorter than the Coronet.

In 1966, the Hemi engine came in a wide variety of models, including this Coronet Deluxe two-door sedan. Looking more like grandma's grocery-getter, this sedan surprised more than a few people on the street.

The April 1966 issue of *Car and Driver* featured a road test of a new Hemi-powered Plymouth Satellite. In the article's opening paragraph, the writer makes reference to the previous month's edition, in which the magazine compared six of the hottest new "Super Cars." Unfortunately, the Hemi wasn't delivered in time for that issue's test. If it had been, it would have resoundingly trounced every car there. "Without cheating, without expensive NASCAR mechanics, without towing or trailing the Plymouth to the test-track," the writer said, "it went faster, rode better, stopped better, and caused fewer problems than all six of the cars tested last month." It was interesting to note that prior to the test, the Hemi Satellite had been driven by magazine staffers from Detroit to New York and then used as a daily driver for a week. The only complaints about the new Plymouth were the location of the tachometer (on the console) and the less-than-impressive styling. The demand was high for

For 1966 the entire Dodge line was restyled. The Coronet 500 was the top-of-the-line model, but compared to its 1966 muscle-car contemporaries, it lacked panache.

Plymouth's new Hemi power, and more than 1,500 were sold in Belvedere I, Belvedere II, and Satellite models in 1966.

The Plymouth Belvedere and Dodge Coronet returned in 1967 with only a few changes to the grille and taillights, but the new top-of-the-line models, the Plymouth GTX and the Dodge R/T, made their debuts. The GTX was Plymouth's first shot at musclecar styling, and it was dead center on target. Available only in a two-door hardtop or convertible, the 1967 GTX featured twin nonfunctional hood scoops. A quick-fill racing style gas cap

The 1966 Plymouth Belvedere/Satellite models, like the Dodges, were restyled. The availability of the Hemi engine in showroom models, like this Belvedere convertible, allowed NASCAR competitors like Richard Petty to race Hemi-powered cars on the track.

was prominent on the left quarter panel. Dual sport stripes and chrome road wheels were optional. When they were added, the GTX had the sporty styling musclecar buyers were looking for. The 440-ci V-8 producing 375 horsepower was standard. The 426 Hemi was optional, but it came with a heavy-duty suspension. The GTX's interior featured saddle-grain vinyl with an attractive tooled leather insert on the seats. Front bucket seats with a center console were standard, and the rear seats were styled to look like bucket seats. The GTX sold well and 125 Hemis made up a fraction of the total of 12,690 units that reached dealers. In the 1967 Plymouth line of Belvederes, Satellites, and GTXs,

there were just slightly fewer than 200 equipped with the Hemi engine.

Dodge introduced its own version of the musclecar, the R/T (Road and Track). The R/T was a Dodge version of the Plymouth GTX. It featured a grille that was similar in styling to that of the Charger's, but the Dodge R/T's headlights were exposed. Three large nonfunctional louvers adorned the center of the hood. Available in only two-door hardtop and convertible body styles, the R/T rode on a heavy-duty suspension. Bucket seats were standard and chrome road wheels were optional. The R/T also featured the 375-horsepower 440 as standard equipment. In 1967, street Hemi

The 426 Hemi engine installed in the 1966 Coronets and Belvederes was a detuned version of the race Hemi that had a lowered compression ratio of 10.25:1 and a milder cam. The only transmissions available were a four-speed manual and a heavy-duty TorqueFlite.

Announcing the Hemi 426 Plymouth Belvedere

**Now what this country needs
is a dragstrip with a couple of
good hairpin curves.**

The Hemi-powered Plymouth Belvedere: a high-performance 426-cubic-inch hemispherical-head V-8. Dual four-barrel carbs. Dual-breaker distributor. High-lift, high-overlap cam. Special plugs, pistons and double valve springs. Low back pressure dual exhaust

system. Blue Streak Special tires. Wide-rim wheels. Oversize front torsion bars. Sway bar. Added-leaf, high-rate rear springs. Firm-Ride shocks.
   And every Belvedere Satellite has: Front bucket seats. Center console with glove box. Deep-pile carpeting.

Padded instrument panel. Safety-Rim wheels. 3-speed automatic or 4-on-the-floor stick, optional.
   Like an iron fist in a velvet glove, the Hemi 426 Plymouth Belvedere.

PLYMOUTH DIVISION **CHRYSLER** MOTORS CORPORATION

Plymouth ...a great car by Chrysler Corporation.

In 1966, the marketing staff at Plymouth didn't waste any time advertising the new Hemi engine's availability or its performance potential. Plymouth placed ads like this one touting the new Belvedere in enthusiast magazines.

engines were installed in 283 Dodge R/Ts, and 117 Hemi engines were installed in the balance of the 1967 Coronet line. While the 1967 Plymouth GTX and Dodge Coronet R/T were outstanding musclecars, complete performance and styling packages (à la GTO and SS396) for the B-body Dodge and Plymouth B-bodies would have to wait until 1968.

In 1968, with one giant leap, Chrysler made a major advancement in the musclecar wars with the release of the new Road Runner. It was the shot in the arm Plymouth needed. The 1967 GTX with all the musclecar options cost considerably more and never had the streetwise look of the GTO. Plymouth decided to strip its newly restyled mid-size entry of any frills, then add a performance engine package and a whimsical cartoon name. With the Road Runner, Plymouth had a low-priced factory hot rod that was capable of kicking any GTO's butt at any stoplight.

The 1968 Plymouth line included the base Belvedere, Road Runner, and GTX. They were all restyled in a smoother, more integrated look. The wheelbase remained at 116 inches, but the track width, front and rear, increased by one-half inch. The GTX also came with bucket seats, a center console, and lots of imitation wood-grain trim. The exterior featured extra chrome trim along the rocker panel and around the wheel openings. A few inches above the rocker panel were two horizontal

The 1967 Plymouth GTX was the first Hemi car whose appearance equaled its performance. Nonfunctional hood scoops were standard on the GTX, but the sport stripes were optional.

The 1967 GTX's stylish interior had front buckets and a chrome center console in which the tachometer was mounted. The "Inland" shifter, named for its manufacturer, selected the gears for the four-speed transmission. It wasn't until 1968 that Hurst shifters became standard equipment.

body stripes that terminated with a large GTX chrome emblem just in front of the rear wheel opening. The GTX's hood featured twin side-facing vents within which the engine size was inset in small chrome letters. Drive-in restaurant regulars and musclecar enthusiasts knew that the 1967 GTX came with a standard 440-ci engine, as did the 1968 model. Once again, the Hemi engine was an option and 446 was so equipped.

Opposite
Chrome road wheels were an option on the 1967 GTX, but red line tires were standard. In addition to the Hemi badges on the front fender, there was a small one on the rear edge of the deck lid.

The 1967 Plymouth GTX had clean sculpted sides that made an exciting styling package. The racing style gas cap on the left quarter panel was also part of the GTX package.

The 1967 GTX was available in either a hardtop or a convertible. Although the 1967 models used the same sheet metal as the 1966, the grille was modified to accept quad headlights. Dale Amy

As nice as the GTX was, the Road Runner got all the press in 1968. Its beauty was in its simplicity. Stripped of all extra chrome, it looked as docile as a librarian's sedan. The Road Runner was initially introduced as a two-door coupe. The hardtop would be introduced later in the model year, but

The 1967 GTX was touted as Plymouth's "Supercar." The standard engine was a 440 with a TorqueFlite, and the only optional engine was the Hemi. Even though Plymouth had finally put together a true musclecar package, the GTXs didn't sell well. A total of 2,500 GTXs were sold in 1967 and only 125 were equipped with the Hemi. This GTX convertible is one of 17 built. Dale Amy

The 1967 R/T featured the same grille as the Charger but without the hidden headlights. On top of the hood were three large simulated louvers. This Hemi-powered R/T convertible was one of only two built in 1967.

no convertible Road Runner models were offered in 1968. The grille was the same egg crate design as the Belvedere, but it was accented in black. The Road Runner used the same hood—with side-facing nonfunctional vents—as the GTX. A small chrome plate near the front edge of the doors discreetly announced that this was a Road Runner. To the rear of this Road Runner emblem was a small decal of the crafty little bird at warp speed. A standing version of the bird was placed on the Road Runner's deck lid. As the year progressed, a decor group was added to the Road Runner, which included a deck lid decal featuring the bird at full speed, trailed by a cloud of dust.

The Road Runner's bench seat interior was initially offered in blue, parchment, or black and silver. When Plymouth introduced the Decor Group, it added gold, red, green, black, and white to the interior color list. Bucket seats were not a Road Runner option in 1968.

The standard engine for the Road Runner was a special version of the 383, producing 335 horsepower and 425 foot-pounds of torque. A four-speed transmission was standard, and a column-shifted TorqueFlite was optional. There was only one optional engine for the 1968 Road Runner—the Hemi. Like the 383, the Hemi came standard with a four-speed, but the TorqueFlite was a no-cost

In 1967 Dodge introduced its new performance model, the R/T (Road and Track). Like the GTX, it came standard with a 440 engine and a host of heavy-duty performance-oriented features. And like the GTX, the only optional engine was the 425-horsepower 426 Hemi.

option. The Performance Axle Package, which included the Dana Sure-Grip rear axle, was a required option. Along with the Hemi engine option came a larger radiator, power front disc brakes, and 15-inch wheels with F-70 Polyglas tires. In 1968, a total of 1,011 customers paid the extra $714 for the Hemi option; of these, 840

Next page
Plymouth's introduction of the Road Runner in 1968 was big news. The finely trimmed GTX was still available, and it featured the same hood as the Road Runner with side-facing nonfunctional scoops. The GTX also had twin body side stripes that terminated at the GTX emblem on the quarter panel. Mopar Muscle

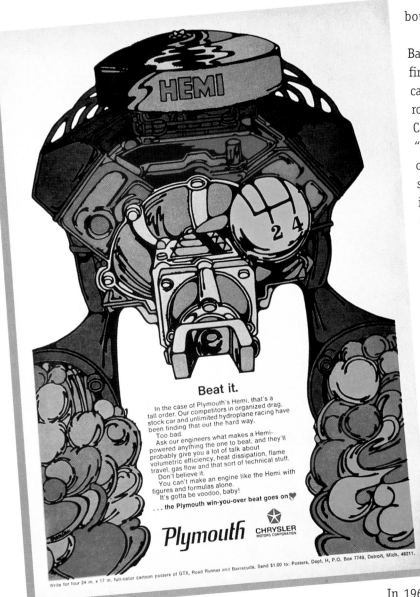

In the case of Plymouth's Hemi, that's a tall order. Our competitors in organized drag, stock car and unlimited hydroplane racing have been finding that out the hard way.

Too bad.

Ask our engineers what makes a Hemi-powered anything the one to beat, and they'll probably give you a lot of talk about volumetric efficiency, heat dissipation, flame travel, gas flow and that sort of technical stuff.

Don't believe it.

You can't make an engine like the Hemi with figures and formulas alone.

It's gotta be voodoo, baby!

... the Plymouth win-you-over beat goes on ♥

Plymouth CHRYSLER MOTORS CORPORATION

Write for four 24 in. x 17 in. full-color cartoon posters of GTX, Road Runner and Barracuda. Send $1.00 to: Posters, Dept. H, P.O. Box 7749, Detroit, Mich. 48211.

The artwork of Peter Max was fashionable in the late 1960s. Plymouth took advantage of it in this slick Hot Rod magazine advertisement to promote the Hemi engine.

bought coupes and 171 bought hardtops.

In the early and mid-1960s, Charlie Di Bari was the spark plug who provided the fire to the successful *Melrose Missile* race car program. The Di Bari family owned Melrose Motors and soon became the northern California Mopar high-performance Mecca. "Shortly after the Road Runners came out," recalls Di Bari, "we wanted to do something that would create a stir, calling more attention to the car and to the dealership. At that time, if you had a minimum of five cars, you could have any car painted a special color. We had five Road Runners painted Omaha Orange. They came in and went right out! We didn't want to have all orange cars, so then we had some painted school bus yellow and then a bright green color. Those were the first three, and the most dominant, of the special colors we came up with." The brightly colored Road Runners were an immediate hit, and soon customers were clamoring for them. Plymouth's marketing personnel in Detroit saw how fast the market was scooping them up. Vivid colors were formerly reserved for trucks but were now part of Chrysler's new musclecar palette.

In 1968 the mid-size muscle market was filled with a host of competitors. Fresh designs and a long list of performance options were what it took to stay in the game. Dodge reskinned its Coronet with slippery sheet metal that featured sculpted quarter panels. The successful R/T option returned in both hardtop and convertible models. With the R/T, the customer had the choice of side stripes or

HEMI ROAD RUNNER: 0-105 IN 13.5 SECS.! ONE OF THE REASONS MOTOR TREND NAMED IT...

CAR OF THE YEAR

See facts, figures, NHRA acceleration times — Page 127.

Bumblebee stripes. The standard engine for the R/T was the 440-ci engine. In 1968, 220 Dodge R/Ts were sold with the Hemi engine.

The big news for Dodge in 1968 was the release of the Super Bee option, which hit the Dodge showrooms in February 1968. It was designed to be a low-priced performance car in the same mold as the 1968 Road Runner. Based on the 440 coupe, the Super Bee featured swing-out quarter windows and had the same power-bulge hood as the R/T. Bumblebee stripes and a circular Super Bee logo on the quarter panel appeared on the rear of the car. The Super Bee's standard engine and transmission was a 335-horsepower 383, backed by a four-speed. The Hemi was optional and 125 were delivered in 1968.

In 1969, the Road Runner was named Motor Trend *magazine's Car of the Year. Never missing a chance to stomp the competition on the street, track, or in print ads, the marketing staff at Plymouth proudly heralded the announcement. The text of the ad went on to describe the quarter-mile times a stock Hemi Road Runner clocked, and the few simple modifications required to improve those times.*

In 1969, the Road Runner returned with a vengeance. Plymouth sold 80,000, almost double the previous year's total. Only minor changes were made to the 1969 model's grille and taillights. The Road Runner was still the low-priced performance king, but the price was increasing and the option

Carter AFB Carburetors

Most gearheads consider the Carter AFB to be the first true performance carburetor. Compact and simple in design, it was the carburetor of choice for the early Mopar and GM musclecars. Carter AFBs were also fitted to the Street Hemi engines.

The Carter Carburetor Company was founded in 1909 by Will Carter. Old Will was a born tinkerer and inventor who had only five years of formal education. In 1910, Carter patented his Model C carburetor. It was an updraft design with three distinct circuits for low, intermediate, and high speeds. In 1911, the company produced the first downdraft carburetor. Starting in 1925, Carter carburetors began showing up as standard equipment on a variety of production cars and trucks. In 1952, Carter released the world's first four-barrel carburetor designated the WCFB (Will Carter Four Barrel). It was constructed from three separate castings and weighed 18 pounds. Archaic by today's standards, the WCFB was a turning point in high-performance fuel delivery systems. It first saw Mopar musclecar action atop the 1957 Chrysler Hemi 392-ci engine.

The WCFB was a wonderful carburetor, but it only flowed at 385 cfm, too little for the emerging large displacement engines. In 1957, Carter introduced its AFB (Aluminum Four Barrel). Depending on the model, it flowed 450 or 625 cfm. The new AFBs soon started popping up in single or dual configurations on a number of Mopar and General Motors musclecar engines.

The new AFB featured a two-piece design cast from aluminum. It was much lighter than the WCFB and flowed better. Like the WCFB, the AFB had a mechanical link between the primary butterfly shaft and the secondary butterfly shaft. This allowed for positive opening of the secondary butterflies. The secondary side also featured an air valve. This air valve temporarily restricted air flow through the secondary butterflies until the engine could use the extra air/fuel mixture available. The air valve increased driveability by eliminating the bog that would take place by the sudden opening of the secondaries. All carburetors have a system for enriching the mixture when under full-throttle conditions. Most other carburetors have what is commonly called a power valve. The Carter AFB has a pair of metering rods that serve that function. Under normal conditions, these rods restrict the flow of fuel through the main metering jets. Under full throttle, when vacuum is at its lowest, the rods are pulled out of the jets, allowing for greater fuel flow. It's a simple system that has a great degree of flexibility for those who wish to fine-tune their carburetors. The rods can be changed for a richer or leaner mixture in a matter of minutes, without taking the carburetor apart.

Carter AFBs first appeared on the cross-ram manifolds of the (modern day) Hemi engines in 1964, but were quickly supplanted by Holleys. When the street Hemi was released in 1966, the Carter AFB was the carburetor of choice. The AFB's compact size allowed it to be comfortably mounted in tandem. The rear carburetor is the primary of the pair and has a choke. Its primary barrels are nearly centrally located on the intake manifold and feed the entire engine under normal low-speed operation. The front carburetor is the secondary of the pair and is connected by what Chrysler called "staged linkage" (hot-rodders know this type of linkage as progressive). This linkage allows the front carburetor to sit idle until it's needed. When the throttle is all the way to the floor, both carburetors are wide open.

Carter AFBs were the only carburetors used on the street Hemi. The rear carburetor had a choke and was used for low-speed operation. At full throttle, both carburetors opened up to provide maximum performance.

The 1969 Road Runner was available in three body styles: a two-door coupe, a hardtop (shown), and a convertible. The cartoon character adorned each door and the center of the deck lid. Also on the left side of the deck lid was a small Hemi emblem. The 15-inch wheels were standard with the Hemi option.

list was expanding. A convertible Road Runner joined the coupe and hardtop models. Power windows, center console, and bucket seats were new to the option list. Standard on any Hemi and optional for the 383, was a Fresh Air hood. This hood was also used on the GTX. It was similar to the hood on

the 1968 Road Runner, except the vents were vertical. Extending under the hood was a system of ductwork that directed fresh air to the engine. Added to the 1969 Road Runner engine option list was the three two-barrel carburetor-equipped 440. Dubbed the 440 Six-Barrel, it came with a nasty-looking black scooped hood and many of the Hemi's heavy-duty suspension components. This powerful engine offered Hemi-style acceleration at half the cost.

Motor Trend magazine selected the 1969 Road Runner as the Car of the Year. In multi-page ads celebrating the fact, Plymouth copywriters went on to give the specific numbers the potential buyers wanted to hear—quarter-mile times and speeds. In stock form, a 1969 Hemi Road Runner, equipped with a TorqueFlite and 4.10 rear axle, consistently ran the quarter-mile in the mid-13-second range at speeds of 105 miles per hour. The next day, the same car was brought back to the track with a few bolt-on performance additions. A Racer Brown cam and kit were added along with a set of Hooker headers. Run with the headers open, the Hemi Road Runner's elapsed times dropped by seven-tenths of a second and speeds improved by five miles per hour.

While overall sales of the 1969 Road Runner increased, the number of buyers opting for the Hemi decreased slightly. The hardtops led the list with 422 Hemis, followed by the coupes at 356, and the convertibles at a lowly 10.

Like the Road Runner, the 1969 GTX saw only minor changes. The grille was redesigned and a GTX emblem was added to the center. In the rear, the taillights were recessed. The body side stripes and chrome molding were removed from the rocker panel and replaced with a flat black lower-body treatment. The GTX shared the Road Runner's Fresh Air hood on its standard 440 and optional Hemi. The success of the Road Runner took a bite out of GTX sales, with only 15,608 units delivered in 1969, which was down 3,300 units compared to 1968 sales. Hemi sales were down accordingly, with only 198 hardtops and 11 convertibles delivered.

In 1968, many options were added to the Road Runner, including bucket seats. An 8000-rpm tachometer was integrated into the right side of the instrument cluster. If someone forgot what model of car they were riding in, all they had to do was look at the right side of the instrument panel to see the smirking face of the little bird.

The 1969 Dodge performance lineup made very few changes to the R/T and Super Bee from their 1968 models. Bumblebee stripes on both models were revised to a single broad stripe. Both the R/T and Super Bee were available with an optional pair of dummy side scoops, which were attached to the leading edge of the quarter panel. The Super Bee, only available as a two-door coupe previously, was now available in a hardtop, and bucket seats were an option. The most significant change for both models was the addition of the Ram Charger hood. Standard with the Hemi and optional with other performance engines, the Ram Charger hood fed fresh air to the carburetors. On the surface of the hood were attached two forward-facing wedge-shaped scoops. Under the hood was a large fiberglass fixture that fed fresh air to the air cleaner. Models with the optional Hemi engine had HEMI

In 1970, both the Plymouth and Dodge were restyled. The Dodge's dual loop grille received mixed reviews, and Plymouth R/Ts featured nonfunctional quarter panel scoops and twin hood scoops that were functional. When the model was equipped with a 426 engine, a small HEMI emblem was placed on each hood scoop.

spelled out in small chrome letters on the outboard side of each scoop. In 1969, a total of 258 Super Bees and 107 Coronet R/Ts were equipped with the Hemi engine.

In 1970 the Dodge Coronet was restyled with a unique front-end treatment. The grille had a wide split in the center, and each side was fitted with a halo-style bumper that tapered as it reached toward that split. It had the look of someone with large nostrils scowling. This would be the final year for the Coronet R/T and Super Bee. In 1971 both of these models would be listed as Charger options.

But in 1970, R/T and Super Bee meant performance. The R/T was available in both hardtop and convertible body styles, whereas the Super Bee was available only in a two-door coupe or hardtop. The R/T side scoop was redesigned with a single forward-facing opening. Bumblebee stripes were again part of the R/T and Super Bee option and could be deleted. With the 1970 Super Bee, the customer could opt for an alternate set of stripes, known as the "reverse C-stripes." They were two hockey stick-style stripes that traced the quarter panel character lines. A larger circular Super Bee decal was placed at the point where they met on the rear of the quarter panel. With the Hemi option, on both the R/T and Super Bee, the Ram Charger hood was standard. The musclecar insurance crackdown was in full swing in 1970, and performance cars including the R/T and Super Bee suffered. Sales in 1970 for the Super Bee were 15,506 units and 2,615 for the R/T. A mere 38 1970 Super Bees were sold with the Hemi option. Hemi-equipped 1970 R/Ts are even more rare, with just 14 sold, and only 1 of those was a convertible. These would be the last Coronet-based cars available with the Hemi engine, and the only mid-size Dodge Hemis sold in 1971 would be Charger Super Bee and Charger R/T models.

The 1970 Road Runner and GTX models were also restyled and were a little more mainstream compared to the 1970 Dodge Coronet. Plymouth's designers were able to use the roof and doors from the 1969 model and add new quarter panels, taillight treatment, and new front-end sheet metal for a fresh look. The quarter panels featured more-rounded corners and had a small nonfunctional scoop on the leading edge. The twin vertical vents were removed from the hood, and a power dome was added. The new Air Grabber scoop was standard on the Hemi-equipped GTXs and Road Run-

The 1970 Dodge R/T's interior was well appointed. A wood-grain and chrome console divided the two standard high-back bucket seats covered in Shallow Elk grain vinyl. The instrument panel also featured wood grain appliqués. The two large dials on the left side of the instrument cluster are the speedometer and tachometer/clock combination.

ners. The driver could flip a switch under the instrument panel that would open the trap door Air Grabber scoop. Wonderfully creative graphics on the side of the scoop would then be visible as outside air was directed to the engine. This scoop won big style points on the street.

The 15-inch wheels, which had been a standard part of the GTX and Road Runner Hemi package, were no longer required, and all Hemis came standard with 14x6-inch wheels, with the 15-inch wheels becoming an option. The Road Runner was available in a two-door coupe, hardtop, or convertible. The GTX, available only as a hardtop, had a twin body stripe that started at the leading edge of the front fender and swept rearward into the quarter panel scoop. Like their brothers over in the Dodge camp, the Plymouth executives were able to

The completely restyled 1971 Road Runner had the rounded look of the new body that made the car look larger than it actually was. When a Hemi was ordered, an Air Grabber hood scoop was included in the center of the domed hood. The Hemi engine was indicated by decals above the side marker light. Dale Amy

read the writing on the wall—musclecar mania was winding down. In 1970, only 152 buyers specified a Hemi engine in the Road Runner, and GTX customers were just as reluctant, buying only 72 Hemis.

In 1971, the only Hemi B-body was the Plymouth Road Runner and GTX. The Belvedere name was dropped and all two-door models were hardtops that were now called Satellite Sebrings. Ply-

mouth offered no convertible in 1971. Both the 1971 Road Runner and GTX were based on this fully redesigned Satellite Sebring. The new Plymouth offerings and the Dodge Chargers now shared the same 115-inch platform, although the Plymouth body was 2.2 inches shorter. The new body appeared larger and more rounded than the 1970 model. The front end had a long, low hood line that extended out to a flush fitting halo-style

Aggressive front and rear wheel-opening flares highlighted the clean styling of the 1971 Road Runner. Road Runner graphics were placed on the quarter panel just above the wheel opening and enclosed in a circle on the right side of the deck lid. Only 55 Road Runners were equipped with the Hemi engine in 1971, the last year of production. Dale Amy

bumper. The grille and headlights were sunk deeply into the bumper. The full wheel openings were flared out slightly. This feature, along with a wider track, gave the new Road Runner and GTX a very aggressive look. Both the GTX and Road Runner offered body-colored bumpers as an option, and a transverse strobe stripe was optional for the Road Runner. It ran from the rear wheel opening forward across the C-pillar and roof and then back down the C-pillar to the other rear wheel opening. With the Hemi engine, the Air Grabber hood was again standard.

In 1971, the curtain officially came down on the musclecar era. A total of 55 Hemi-powered Road Runners and 35 Hemi-powered GTXs were sold that year. Emission constraints and auto insurance surcharges had finally sucked the oxygen out of the musclecar atmosphere.

2

The Winged Wonders and Chargers

Charger, Charger Daytona, Plymouth Superbird

Chrysler's management was unhappy with the public's poor response to the 1962 Plymouths and Dodges. Sales for that year were dismal compared the rest of the industry. Chrysler's management wanted its cars to have a cleaner, more mainstream design. Elwood Engle, a Ford designer, was hired to replace Virgil Exner, Chrysler's premier designer during the 1950s. Engle was given the formidable task of reshaping Chrysler's look and doing it in minimal time. To make Engle's task more monumental, two new cars were added, the Plymouth Barracuda and the Dodge Charger.

The Dodge Charger was conceived as an upscale personal luxury car in the same mode as the Buick Riviera, Olds Toronado, and Ford Thunderbird, but less costly. The new Charger was to lead the Dodge

Continued on page 39

In 1970, the final year for the second-generation Dodge Charger, the Charger R/T had large rear-facing scoops added to the doors. The placement of the scoops required the relocation of the HEMI badges from the doors to the front fenders. Dale Amy

Heading the Dodge Rebellion advertising program in 1966 was the smartly styled Charger. It was built on the Coronet platform, and Chrysler designers incorporated a full-width grille that cleverly disguised its hidden headlights and parking lights in amongst the vertical bars.

A full-length console, mounting an optional clock, split both the 1966 Charger's front and rear bucket seats. The chrome instrument panel's two center pods contained the 150 mile per hour speedometer and the 6,000-rpm tachometer.

Four V-8 engines were available in the 1966 Charger, including the 426 Hemi. In 1966, all Hemi engines came with a large chrome-plated air cleaner and black crinkle-painted valve covers. Adjusting the valve lash was a lengthy project because items like heater hoses had to be removed in order to take off the large valve cover.

The 1966 Charger's full-width taillight matched the design theme of the front end, and the rear window's outer edges curled up to meet the sweeping roof line.

For the second-generation Dodge Charger, Chrysler designers were determined to create a car that looked completely different from the Coronet. Their vision was a car that looked as though it could be driven directly from the street to the high banks of Daytona. The new Charger featured a wedge-shape body, fastback roofline, and aggressive bulges around each full wheel opening. Dale Amy

Continued from page 35

Rebellion advertising theme in presenting a new image of performance and clean, inventive design.

The 1966 Charger shared its platform with the 117-inch wheelbase Coronet. Both cars shared the front- and side-sheet metal, but the Charger's fastback roof line dramatically set it apart. Because of the Charger's hardtop design, a considerable amount of body structure had to be added in the areas of the C-pillars and the upper rear deck. Dodge designers made small but significant changes to the Coronet's quarter panels. The rear wheel openings were enlarged and shaped the same as the front wheel openings, which gave the Charger an aggressive, sporty stance. The leading edge of the quarter panels received two horizontal depressions that simulated air intakes. The sides of the Charger were clean and devoid of any trim other than a thin belt line molding, a rocker panel molding, and thin wheel lip moldings. The large triangular sail panel was accented with a tasteful CHARGER name plate.

The Charger's front-end treatment was also bold. Within the large rectangular opening was a full-width grille with hidden headlights. The grille consisted of a series of thin vertical chrome bars, whose density concealed the split lines for the headlight doors and the parking lights. Even when the headlight doors were open, the lights were fully trimmed. It was a small detail that few manufacturers took time to master with hidden headlights. One plague that afflicts cars with hidden headlights are doors that fail to open or close completely. This "lazy eye" look neutralizes the overall effect of hidden headlights and makes noncustomers out of potential customers. Chrysler engineers were given the job of designing a fail-proof mechanism. To accomplish this, they gave each light its own heavily geared electric motor.

Mr. Norm's Hemi Charger

In 1968, Dodge high performance dealer extraordinaire, Norm "Mr. Norm" Kraus, drove a new Hemi-powered Charger R/T. "I had a '68 Charger street Hemi with a pearl paint job—it was gorgeous," recalls Kraus. The technicians at Grand Spaulding Dodge were always experimenting with cams and other engine components and Kraus' Charger was one of the test beds. "I wanted a top-end cam because I lived 25 miles from the dealership and spent a lot of time on the expressway. We also curved the distributor and put a set of headers on the car, but I never ran them open. I always felt the engine breathed a little better with the headers. A lot of guys tried to egg me on to race them. They knew who I was and the route I took to work. I'd be cruisin' in my Charger listening to the music, and I'd look to my left, and here's a guy pointing (giving the all-American signal for "Do you want to race?"). I really frowned upon street racing, but every once in a while I'd have to see how well our engine package worked. I'd inch 'em up saying no-no-no. So instead of going 55, now we were at 65. Then I'd nod and we'd both hit it. That Hemi would take off—it was something beautiful. That Charger was a great street car. Gas at that time was pennies compared to now, so you didn't care about the mileage. I always drove a Hemi and enjoyed it."

The modifications made to the 1969 Dodge Charger 500 were designed for NASCAR competition. The grille was pulled forward, flush to the edge of the opening. The hidden headlights were dropped in favor of exposed quad units, and the A-pillars received a special piece of bright trim.

When the driver pulled the light switch, a red light illuminated on the instrument panel until the headlight doors were fully open. An override switch was provided to open the doors in icy weather or to clean the headlight lenses.

The rear of the Charger carried the same wide rectangular one-piece look as the front. Within a thin chrome molding was a large single taillight lens. Widely spaced individual chrome letters spelled out CHARGER across the width of the lens. The 1966 Charger looked long, low, and wide. In addition, the execution of the exterior sheet metal and details was crisp and contemporary.

The Charger's interior was as fashionable as its exterior. It featured individual seating for four. The front seats were Chryslers new clamshell-design buckets. The rear seats were also buckets, with backrests that could fold down, converting the

In the rear, the Daytona 500's rear window was blended flush with the C-pillars, creating a smooth flow of air over the roof. The rear window placement and subsequent roof modifications required a severe shortening of the deck lid. The taillight treatment and quick release-style gas cap were standard on all Chargers, but the transverse Bumblebee stripes were only on the Charger 500.

small luggage compartment into one of extended length. Splitting the seats was a full-length console, trimmed with a die-cast chrome plate with a brushed aluminum appliqué. At the forward end, a clock was mounted in a chrome housing. In keeping with the sporty theme, all 1966 Dodge Chargers with optional engines came with a floor-mounted shifter for either the TorqueFlite automatic or four-speed manual transmission. The instrument panel held four large chrome-rimmed pods. The two pods in the center housed the speedometer and a 6,000 rpm tachometer.

Dodge defined the Charger's performance image with the selection of standard and optional engines. The 318-ci 230-horsepower V8 was the base engine, and the 361- and 383-ci engines and the 426-ci street Hemi were optional. Along with the Hemi engine came a heavy-duty suspension, which featured 11-inch brake drums.

Even though it was introduced late in the model year, the 1966 Dodge Charger sold well. Of the 37,344 that were produced, 468 were equipped with the Hemi engine. Drag racers didn't latch onto the Charger like the NASCAR crowd did. The sleek aerodynamics and extra weight were counterproductive to the drag-racing credo. But down South, the good ol' boys of NASCAR saw the advantages of the slick roof line and powerful Hemi engine. David Pearson, driving a Dodge Charger, won the NASCAR Grand National championship.

Even Wile E. Coyote on an Acme rocket sled would have a hard time catching this Lemon Twist-colored Superbird. Based on a 1970 Road Runner, it featured much of the same wind-cheating design tricks that were used on the Daytona 500. All Superbirds came with Rallye wheels.

Only 135 Superbirds were powered by the Hemi engine. The rest of the 2,000 produced were equipped with a 440. Even though all other Hemi-equipped 1970 Road Runners were equipped with the Air Grabber hood, the Superbird was not. The distinctive Road Runner "Beep Beep" horn is at the left edge of the radiator tank. It's painted a shade of light purple and features the smirking face of the bird on a decal that states, "Voice of the Road Runner."

The Superbird's rear window was supported by two angled vertical stabilizers. The PLYMOUTH script on the quarter panel was done in the same font and size as on the side of Richard Petty's race car.

Chrysler didn't want to alter a successful car, and it made only minor changes to the 1967 Charger. The 440-ci engine was added to the option list. But in 1967, sales of the Charger were dismal—less than half those of the previous year. Sales of the Hemi engine dropped even more dramatically, down to 118.

For the 1968 model year, Chrysler designer Bill Brownlie was determined to create a Charger that looked completely different from the Coronet. His vision was a car that could be driven directly to the high banks of Daytona but could also be toured on the street. Design staff members got busy and submitted their renderings to Brownlie. The designer who shared Brownlie's vision was Richard Tighstin, and his sketches showed a car with a narrow front end that got wider toward the rear. Tighstin's side profile showed the car's wedge shape with a built-in rear spoiler. This would be the second-generation Charger.

The new Charger carried many of the same styling cues as the original, including the full-width rectangular grille and large front and rear wheel openings. The body on the new Charger lost its

The roof extension needed to fit the special rear window, which can be seen in the reflection off the driver's side C-pillar. Plymouth installed vinyl tops on all Superbirds to save the enormous amount of expensive metal finishing required to fit the rear window.

High insurance surcharges took their toll on the sales of sleek Charger R/Ts in 1970, when only 10,337 were sold. Of that number, only 112 were equipped with the Hemi engine. Dale Amy

angular lines in favor of a smooth, Coke-bottle shape. The sheet metal at each wheel opening was raised and flared slightly. The black-out grille carried hidden headlights and thin vertical bars similar to the first-generation Charger's grille. The subtle quarter panel scoops on the earlier Charger were moved up to the doors, and an additional set was cut into the hood. Within the scalloped hood

scoops was an optional set of turn indicators. Keeping in sync with the racing theme, Chrysler designers added a large quick-fill gas cap on top of the left quarter panel. The Charger's flat rear window tunneled into the fastback roofline. In the rear, the full-width taillight of the 1966 and 1967 models was dropped in favor of two pairs of circular lights set into an angled panel. The interior of the new

Hidden headlights, formerly standard on the Charger, were now optional. For 1971, the halo-style grille received a center bar. From the angle of this photograph, the Charger's Coke-bottle shape is apparent.

Charger was not as well detailed as the previous model had been. The seats, buckets in front and bench rear, were less supportive, but still attractive. The instrument panel had the efficiency of an aircraft cockpit, with two large dials on the left (clock and 150-mile-per-hour speedometer) and four smaller gauges on the right. An optional tachometer was integrated into the clock.

The chassis and engine combinations for the 1968 Charger were carryovers from 1967. In 1968, a new model was added to the Charger—the R/T

(Road and Track). The R/T was a performance package that offered a standard 375-horsepower 440-ci engine and a host of heavy-duty components. TorqueFlite was the standard transmission, and a four-speed manual was optional. Also standard were rear Bumblebee stripes, but the graphics could be deleted. The Hemi engine was only available with the R/T package, and in 1968 475 were sold.

The 1969 Charger was released with very few changes from the 1968 model, but the most notable change was the addition of a center split in the

Continued on page 51

In 1971 the Dodge Charger and Coronet were merged into one model. Unfortunately, this took away the uniqueness of the Charger, but it didn't diminish its visual appeal. The Charger's new sheet metal had an aggressive rake.

All 1971 Charger R/T models had a distinctive domed hood with flat black graphic and hood pins. All Hemi models had the trapdoor-style Ramcharger hood scoop.

50

The 1971 Charger interiors were tastefully elegant. All R/Ts came with bucket seats covered in El Paso grained vinyl, and the gauges in front of the driver were nestled into a coved area of the instrument panel. The two larger dials housed the 150-mile-per-hour speedometer and 7,000-rpm tachometer.

Continued from page 47

grille. In the rear, a new pair of rectangular-shaped taillights, reminiscent of those on the 1967 Charger, replaced the circular ones. The Hemi engine was again available only with the R/T option, and 432 were delivered in 1969.

Certain aspects of the new Charger's exterior, while stylish, hindered performance. The deep-set

The Charger R/Ts had special three-segment taillight lenses in an argent silver housing. The rear end treatment featured a contoured rear window that swept down to the deck lid and had a small built-in spoiler on the rear lip. This particular R/T also has an optional rear wing spoiler.

Hemi Crate Motors

Want a Hemi engine for your car? No problem—just call up your local Mopar Performance Parts dealer and ask for a Hemi Crate Motor. Two factory-engineered versions are available. The basic 426-ci engine (part number P5249667) uses a cast-iron block with cross-bolted mains. It has forged 9:1 pistons, cast-iron heads, and a hydraulic cam with 278 degrees of duration. With the recommended 750 cfm carburetor and headers, this engine develops an impressive 465 horsepower and 520 foot-pounds of torque.

If that's not enough power, you can step up and order the 528-ci Hemi (part number P4876690). The 102 extra cubes are available through a bore of 4.50 and a stroke of 4.15. This king of the elephant parade blasts out 610 horsepower and 650 foot-pounds of torque. It uses the same block as the lower horsepower version, but is fitted with 10:25 pistons and aluminum heads. To attain that horsepower, the addition of headers and a single four-barrel carburetor that flows between 850–900 cfm is recommended.

Both engines come equipped with a six-quart oil pan, a dual plane single four-barrel intake manifold, stainless steel valves (2.25-inch diameter intake and 1.94-inch diameter exhaust), and a Mopar Performance electronic distributor.

Legendary power doesn't come cheap. At your local Mopar Performance Parts dealer, the 426-ci version lists for $13,750 and the 528 for $16,975. By shopping around, you can save a few thousand through mail order or specialty suppliers.

Buying a Hemi engine is as easy as stopping by your local Mopar Performance Parts dealer. Two versions are available: a 426-ci version that develops 465 horsepower (pictured), or an aluminum-headed stroker version that pumps out 610 horsepower. Mopar Performance

Bumblebee stripes, which had been common on previous Charger R/Ts, were no longer available in 1971. The new stripes, available only in black, wrapped around the cowl and swept down the belt line, terminating at the end of the quarter panel.

The 1971 Super Bee and Dodge R/T were both performance models, but of the two, the Super Bee was the plain vanilla model, having a more businesslike interior, offering fewer frills. The Super Bee's taillights are standard 1971 Charger units.

grille and tunneled rear window were detrimental to high speed. Late in the 1968 model year, Chrysler designed a modified version it named the Charger 500, which would be released as a 1969 model. The Charger 500 featured a flush-mounted grille and a rear window that followed the sloping shape of the C-pillars. This flush-mounted rear window required a special shortened deck lid. A Bumblebee stripe ran across the back, with the

number 500 on the quarter panel. NASCAR required that a minimum of 500 production-line cars be built in order to qualify for competition. The intent of the rule was to eliminate the building of special race-only cars that weren't available to the general public.

The Charger 500s were equipped with a standard 440 engine at a base price of $3,591 or the optional Hemi at an additional $648.20. A Torque-

In 1971, the Coronet was no longer available, and the Super Bee option was only available on the Charger. The Super Bee shared the R/Ts domed hood (with Super Bee graphics) and body stripes. When equipped with a Hemi engine, the script on the side of the hood declared 426 HEMI.

Flite or a four-speed manual were the only two transmissions available. Records show that only 67 Charger 500s were Hemi powered. *Hot Rod* magazine had three of these Hemi-powered Charger 500s available for road tests for its February 1969 issue. Unfortunately, one of the two four-speed cars was stolen just prior to the test. Of the two Hemi 500s, staffer Steve Kelly favored the Torque-Flite-equipped 500. He wrote, "This is the kind of car you make excuses to drive." One option he

heartily recommended was front disc brakes. Both Charger 500s were run at the drags. The four-speed car was equipped with a 4.10 rear axle and ran the best times at 13.48 seconds and a speed of 109 miles per hour. The TorqueFlite was mated to a 3.23 rear axle on the other Hemi Charger 500, and it ran the quarter in 13.8 seconds at a speed of 105 miles per hour.

The Charger 500, with its revised aerodynamics, faced the Torino Talladega and Mercury Cyclone

The trapdoor Ramcharger hood scoop was opened by flipping a switch under the left side of the instrument panel. This activated a vacuum actuator under the hood, opening the scoop. Fresh air would then be ducted to the engine's air filter.

Spoiler with their modified front ends in NASCAR competition. Whatever the Charger 500 had gained in aerodynamics was now equaled by the Fords and Mercurys. To gain the competitive edge, Chrysler pulled out all the stops with the Charger Daytona.

The 1969 Charger Daytona was the most outrageous and infamous of all the Dodge Chargers. It was Chrysler's throw-down-the-gauntlet approach to building an unbeatable car for NASCAR competition. Costs to Chrysler for the Daytona were rumored to be as high as $1 million. The Charger Daytona picked up where the Charger 500 left off. It retained the 500's flush-mounted rear window, but used a new nose piece and rear wing developed in a wind tunnel. The wedge-shaped nose was constructed of sheet metal and added 18 inches to the front of the car. Rear-facing scoops were added to the tops of the front fenders for tire clearance on the race versions. Engineers added a rear spoiler that was 58 inches wide. It was supported by 23.5-inch-high uprights that grew out of the top of the quarter panels. This wing was adjustable, and it canceled the lift created at the rear of the car. The rear of the Charger Daytona was adorned with a wide Bumblebee stripe that covered the wing. Emblazoned in large letters on the quarter panel was the name DAYTONA. These body modifications reduced the aerodynamic drag by 15 percent over the Charger 500, thus greatly enhancing the Charger Daytona's top speed. Chrysler's adventures into the heady world of aerodynamics paid off with a car that could easily reach and maintain speeds of 200 miles per hour. It was also a public relations success. Other than the race cars, only 503 Charger Daytonas were built in 1969, and only 70 of those had the Hemi engine.

The Charger Daytona proved to be an excellent performer on the high banks. When it made its first appearance at NASCAR's Talladega race in September 1969, it quickly became the fastest stock car in history when Charlie Glotzbach took the pole for the Talladega 500 with a speed of 199.466 miles per hour. The anticipated showdown against the Fords didn't materialize. The Ford drivers withdrew, citing unsafe conditions, and Richard Brickhouse won the race in a Charger Daytona.

Legend has it that because of the success of the Charger Daytona, Richard Petty wanted to switch to a Dodge Charger Daytona, but he was under contract to drive a Plymouth. The people at Plymouth refused to let him compete in a Dodge, so Petty defected and drove a Ford for the 1969 season. In 1970, Petty would return behind the wheel of Plymouth's new winged car, the Superbird.

The 1970 Plymouth Superbird had the assertive good looks of the 1969 Charger Daytona. Like its Dodge Daytona brother, the Superbird was built and sold to the general public to comply with NASCAR rules. At first glance it appears as if the Daytona parts were simply bolted onto a Road Runner to create the Superbird, but they weren't. All Superbird components were unique to that car. The extended nosecone, which housed hidden headlights, had a small rubber strip across the front. Just under the leading edge, there was an opening for air to enter the radiator. To fit the nosecone onto the Road Runner, the leading edges of the front fenders and the hood were extended to match the nosecone's surface. The rearward-facing scoops were placed over the front tires and were the same color as the body work. The Superbird's rear window was also unique. Along with roof and rear deck modifications, the rear window

Dual exhausts were standard on the Super Bee, but the rear wing was optional along with the small vertical bumper guards. Documentation showed that this particular 1971 Super Bee was originally delivered from Grand Spaulding Dodge. The owner has taken the time to add the proper Grand Spaulding license plate frame and decal to the deck lid—both status symbols in their day.

was designed to improve aerodynamics. To facilitate the speedy assembly of the street versions, all Superbirds sold to the general public were equipped with a vinyl top. This precluded expensive metal finishing that would have required extra time and expense. Rising from the top of the quarter panels were the uprights that supported the rear wing. The Superbird's uprights

were much wider at the base than those on the Charger Daytona.

All Superbirds came standard with the 440-ci engine with either a single four-barrel carburetor or the six-barrel configuration of three two-barrel Holleys. The Hemi was also optional and 135 Superbirds were so equipped. All Superbirds came with an all vinyl interior in black, or white with black trim.

A bench seat was standard and front bucket seats were optional. The instrumentation was the same as on the 1970 Road Runner. The exterior colors for the Superbird were limited to Alpine White, Petty Blue, Lemon Twist, TorRed, Burnt Orange Metallic, Vitamin C Orange, Limelight, or Blue Fire Metallic. The Superbird's racing culture was distinctively shown by its graphics. On the quarter panel was a large decal that spelled out the word PLYMOUTH in the same size and font as Richard Petty's race car. On the nose and wing uprights was the rambunctious little bird with a racing helmet tucked under its right wing.

In 1970 the Dodge Charger received only minor tweaks. Most notable were the redesigned grille and front bumper. The doors on the R/T received an added reversed scoop, which was located at the forward edge, covering the stamped depressions. Just as in the previous two years, the Hemi engine was available only in the R/T, and just 112 were sold.

In 1971, Dodge restyled the Charger and combined it with the Coronet. The new Charger/Coronet had to retain the aggressive good looks for the musclecar buyer, but also had to be sedate enough for the buyer of a four-door family car. Many enthusiasts believed that the new Charger had lost its individuality, because it shared a four-door platform.

The new Charger had a forward raked look that was attributed to the raised belt line. Although it had a two-inch-shorter wheelbase, the new Charger looked as long as the original. Many of the original Charger styling cues were still in place on the 1971 model. The grille was still rectangular in shape, surrounded by a halo bumper. Hidden headlights, previously standard

on the Charger, were now optional on all but the base Charger. The basic Coke-bottle shape of the body was still there, along with the full wheel openings. The roof didn't have the tunneled rear window, but the deck lid retained a small spoiler.

The R/T and Super Bee were performance models of the 1971 Charger. The R/T featured a domed and louvered hood with flat black accents. When the optional Hemi was ordered, the louvers were dropped in favor of a Ram Charger hood, also optional with the 440 engine. The R/T used unique door outer skins that had two vertical depressions at the door's leading edge. Inside these depressions were tape accents. The R/T also featured a body side stripe that started at the rear edge of the hood and swept along the belt line to the end of the quarter panel. The door accents and body side stripes, which came only in black, could be deleted. Small R/T emblems were added to the sides of the front fenders and to the rear edge of the deck lid. The Charger R/T had a special taillight lens that was divided into three sections per side. In 1971, there were only 63 Dodge Charger R/Ts sold with the Hemi engine.

The Super Bee was the inexpensive hot rod of the Charger lineup, and it came standard with a 300 horsepower 383 with options of a 440 or Hemi. Heavy-duty suspension, wide oval tires, and Rallye wheels were some of the hot standard equipment. Unlike the R/T, the Super Bee was fitted with the standard two-light-per-side Charger taillights. A special Super Bee hood decal was applied to the raised hood dome. The same body stripes ran from the cowl rearward on the R/T. Super Bee emblems were on the side of the front fender and on the back of the deck lid. Only 22 1971 Super Bees were equipped with Hemi engines.

3

Chrysler's Pocket Rockets

Hemi 'Cudas and Challengers

To compete against the Mustang and soon-to-be-introduced Camaro, Chrysler's designers had to offer more than one body style. They also had to make room for larger engines. In the fall of 1966, Plymouth introduced its all-new Barracuda. In addition to the fastback, a coupe and a convertible were added to the lineup. The new Barracuda was longer, wider, and lower than the previous model. It had a muscular look and an engine lineup to match. With the availability of the 383-ci engine, it was the performance equal of Mustangs powered with the 390-ci engine. The 383 was only available with a four-speed manual or TorqueFlite transmission. Even with the two-inch-wider engine compartment, the 383 was a tight fit, and the accessory drive had to be

Performance cars were made to be driven, and driving a Hemi 'Cuda is a definite adrenaline rush. Fat, 60-series tires were standard on the 'Cuda. They complemented the vehicle's overall low and wide design. This 1970 Hemi 'Cuda features the optional Elastomeric bumper and vinyl top.

61

The 1970 'Cuda was an entirely new vehicle and was designated as an E-body car. It was styled to compete against the hot-selling Mustangs and Camaros. It featured the long-nose short-deck design philosophy of its contemporaries.

redesigned. The new Barracuda sheet metal was fitted over the original platform, limiting the space available for a larger engine. Even when the Barracuda was reskinned in 1968, the engine compartment was limited to the 383. The only exceptions were the purpose-built drag race Hemi Barracudas.

In 1967, the musclecar boom experienced a sharp incline. At that time Chrysler's Advanced Styling Studios began work on what would eventually become the 1970 Barracuda. They worked in concert with the engineering groups to design a car with an engine compartment large enough to accommodate a 440 with air conditioning or a

Hemi. In the musclecar wars, there was no substitute for cubic inches, and Chrysler was determined to build the most potent pony car ever.

To build such a car, an entirely new platform had to be created—the E-body. The larger B-body (Coronet/Charger) cowl was used as the starting point. The front sub frame and rear axle were also borrowed. (It is interesting to note that Camaro was constructed from Nova components in Chevy's parts bins.) The Advanced Styling group packaged the vehicle, determining wheelbase, seating positions, greenhouse, and door sills. With those parameters approved, the package was given to the Plymouth styling group. It was at this time that Chrysler management decided to build a Dodge equivalent—the Challenger. The Challenger would be positioned in the market as the upscale model to compete against the Mercury Cougar and Pontiac Firebird. While appearing similar to the Barracuda, the Challenger would be quite different.

Both cars shared the upper body and the basic design theme of the long, low front end and an aggressive short, kicked-up rear deck. Only two body styles were to be built, a notch-back coupe and a convertible. A fastback wasn't in the

The 1970 Dodge Challenger was built on the same E-body platform as the 'Cuda. While similar in appearance to the 'Cuda, its body was unique and rode on a slightly longer wheelbase.

The sleek new E-bodies carried all the latest design trends, which included flush door handles, streamlined racing style mirrors, and hidden windshield wipers. Protruding through the hood on all Hemi-powered 'Cudas was the Shaker hood scoop.

The 1970 'Cudas and Challengers were only available in two-door hardtop (often called a notch back) and convertible body styles. The new E-bodies were two inches lower and five inches wider than the 1969 models.

Optional on the 1970 'Cuda were "hockey stick" stripes. These stripes accented the rear quarter panel, terminating with the engine's cubic-inch displacement near the taillight. When a 'Cuda was equipped with a Hemi, the stripes simply spelled out HEMI.

cards. The Challenger's wheelbase was 110 inches, 2 inches longer than the Barracuda. The height was just a fraction over 50 inches, 2 inches lower than the previous Barracuda. Both cars, however, were low and wide. The new Barracuda's width was 74.7 inches, an increase of 5 inches over the previous model. The Challenger was even wider, at 76.1 inches. This width gave the E-bodied cars an exceptionally aggressive look from the front or rear. This look was accentuated with the addition of the fat 60-series Polyglas tires. When equipped with narrower standard tires, the E-bodies looked sadly out of proportion. The Challenger was longer at 191.3 inches compared to the Barracuda's 186.7 inches. Both cars offered full wheel openings, with the Challenger's more elliptical in shape than the Barracuda's. The Barracuda carried a soft horizontal character line down the side. The Challenger's body character line was more pronounced and it rose up over the rear wheel opening. It also flared out slightly, which can be attributed to the Challenger's dimensionally wider girth. The sides of both bodies tucked under severely in an area called "tumble home" by body designers. Both cars had flush door handles, hidden wipers, and ventless door glass—all the latest design trends coming out of the Detroit studios. The Challenger, true to its upscale image, had more bright trim, including thin wheel-opening moldings.

The front and rear of the new Challenger and Barracuda were also unique. Both were clean and classy designs. The Barracuda's oval-shaped grille had a single center peak accentuated by a series of deep-set horizontal bars. A pair of headlights was located at the outboard ends. The rolled-under valence panel below the thin horizontal bumper was painted body color, with an elliptical center opening allowing fresh air to the radiator. The Challenger also had a thin horizontal bumper. Below the bumper, the opening in the body color valence panel was more rectangular. The deep-set mesh grille was accentuated with a thin rectangular chrome molding. Two quad headlights were at the outboard ends. The parking lights on the Barracuda were neatly blended into the upper portion of the grill, whereas the Challenger's circular parking lights were tunneled into the valence panel.

The Plymouth designers wanted a full urethane front end for the new Barracuda, similar to the '68 GTO, but unfortunately, the money wasn't available. What they were able to develop was the Elastomeric bumper option. This was an unchromed bumper with high-density urethane foam molded over the surface. It was then painted body color. The Elastomeric was available for both front or rear, giving the designers their body-color bumpers. This option was only available on the Barracuda.

The rear bumpers on the Barracuda and Challenger were thin horizontal bars with an upturn at each end. Small vertical bumper guards were located near the outboard ends and extended down from the bumper onto the rear valence panel. Depending on the engine option, dual exhaust outlets were carved into the rear valence panel on both cars.

The taillight treatment also differed on both E-body cars. The Barracuda had a flat inset panel that housed the license plate in the center and the taillights at the outboard ends. Each rear light fixture incorporated a backup light and had a pair of thin horizontal bars across the lenses. Because of the license plate location, the Barracuda's deck lid lock was offset to the right.

Chrysler's designers were not restricted to adding a new body to an old platform when creating the new E-body 'Cuda. The 'Cuda's body sides carried a smart horizontal character line and a small lip on the full wheel openings. The 'Cuda's tightly integrated design can be seen in the way the rear valence panel was designed to blend smoothly into the vertical bumper guard.

The 'Cuda's interior featured vinyl-covered high-back bucket seats. Leather seats (as pictured) were an option. This 'Cuda's interior also features an optional three-spoke steering wheel, center console, and "Pistol Grip" shifter.

The Challenger's thin recessed taillight fixture carried the full width of the rear panel and featured a backup light in the center. The position of this light required the license plate to be mounted on the lower valence panel.

Both the Barracuda and Challenger could be ordered in three series. The Barracuda was the base model, followed by the Gran Coupe, and then the sporty 'Cuda. The Challenger also had three series: the base Challenger, the optional SE series, and the R/T (Road and Track).

The 'Cuda was easily identified by its special twin-scoop hood, hood pins, driving lights, Rallye wheels, and flat black taillight panel. An optional "hockey stick" body stripe was available. It slashed along the quarter panel, terminating with the engine's displacement figures in prominent letters or, on the cars equipped with the Hemi engine, the word HEMI.

The Dodge R/T came with a standard power bulge hood that featured twin inlets and hood pins. This hood was available with a special blackout paint treatment. Like the 'Cuda, the R/T also featured white letter tires on Rallye wheels. As part of the R/T package, a rear bumblebee stripe or full-length body stripe was offered at no cost. The body side stripe accented the Challenger's side character line. The Bumblebee stripe had the effect of chopping off the rear of the car.

When ordered with the Hemi engine, the 'Cuda came standard with the Shaker hood scoop (it was optional on 'Cudas equipped with a 340, 383, or 440 engine). This scoop protruded through the hood and, as advertised, shook and shimmied while the engine revved. It had two openings in the front that allowed fresh air to enter the carbs when a lever on the instrument panel opened a valve in the scoop. Interestingly, the Shaker hood scoop was also optional on the Challenger with the Hemi engine. On both the 'Cuda and Challenger, the Shaker hood could be ordered in argent silver, flat black, or body color. The cold air flowing through the scoop enhanced engine performance by a few horsepower. But the visual impact was just as important as the horsepower, especially when everyone was able to see the word HEMI on the side of the scoop.

The catalog of colors for the Barracuda and Challenger was long and kaleidoscopic. Chrysler targeted these cars for the youth market and wanted the colors to be as bright and brazen as the cars themselves. Some of the more catchy colors were TorRed, Lemon Twist, Vitamin C, Sublime, Lime Light, Go-Mango, and of course, Hemi Orange. With the combinations of body styles and series, the addition of body stripes, hood configurations, and tire and wheel combinations, no two cars looked alike.

The interiors of the Barracuda and Challenger were simple but not as well executed as the exterior styling. An excess of plastic tended to make the interior look cheap when compared

The 'Cuda was the performance-oriented model of the 1970 Barracuda line, featuring a standard dual-scooped hood, hood pins, driving lights, and a rear taillight panel painted flat black.

to competitive models, such as the Camaro and Mustang. Typical of the pony cars of the era, the Barracuda and Challenger had front bucket seats and small rear bench seats. The door and quarter trim panels were molded with an integral arm rest. In front of the driver, the padded instrument panel was coved. The three-spoked steering wheel sat high in relation to the driver's seat. This elicited complaints from journalists when first test driving the Barracuda and Challenger.

When the Mustang was introduced in 1964, it was offered with a wealth of options, so the buyer could build the car of his or her dreams. When the Camaro was released, Chevrolet followed the same philosophy, offering a large number of possible option combinations. Chrysler followed suit with the Barracuda and Challenger. The wide array of interior and exterior options included leather seats, center console, Rallye

The parking lights were integrated into the upper grille opening. The deep-set black grille was accented by a single thin horizontal red stripe. Instead of chrome, body-colored Elastomeric bumpers could be specified for the front and rear of the 1970 'Cuda. The small circular driving light below the bumper was standard as part of the 'Cuda package.

The offset trunk-lock cylinder is partially hidden by the 'Cuda nameplate. The lock was placed there because rear design did not permit a center-mounted lock. All 'Cudas featured dual exhaust with bright rectangular tips that extended through the rear valence panel.

wheels, rear window louvers, vinyl roof, and even a vacuum-operated trunk release.

These options continued under the hood. A host of different engines were offered for the Barracuda and Challenger, culminating with the Hemi. At a cost of $1,227, the Hemi option added considerably to the $2,800 base price for each car. When adding the Hemi, many heavy-duty components were included, so the car could keep up with the engine. Only two transmissions were offered with the Hemi option, the TorqueFlite automatic and a four-speed manual. Selecting the gears on the four-speed was done with a Hurst shifter. This shifter didn't use a

The big Hemi engine fits snugly into the E-body engine compartment. This Hemi Challenger R/T is equipped with the optional Shaker hood scoop. The Shaker hood scoops were available in flat black, argent silver, or body color. The chrome emblem on the side of the scoop proudly announces that the engine below is a 426 HEMI.

All 1970 Hemi 'Cudas came equipped with the Shaker hood scoop. The opening to the carburetors was controlled by a lever under the instrument panel. A large rubber seal attached to the scoop sealed the hood, preventing water from entering the engine compartment.

Previous page
All 1970 Hemi 'Cudas came with 15x7 Rallye wheels, extra heavy-duty suspension with special front torsion bars, a large front sway bar, unique heavy-duty rear leaf springs, and a Dana 60 rear axle.

The 1970 E-body Dodge Challenger had a pronounced horizontal character line along the side that rose up over the rear wheel opening. The Challenger's R/T option provided the same level of standard performance options as the 'Cuda.

Added to the front fenders of the 1971 'Cudas were "gills," which were four nonfunctional louvers.

ball or T-handle; instead it used a vertical shift handle initially called a "strip-grip" shifter, which later became known as the "pistol grip" shifter. Barracudas and Challengers with a 440 or a Hemi were equipped with extra heavy-duty front torsion bars and a large diameter (0.94) front stabilizer bar. The rear suspension had an unusual combination of leaf springs. The left side had five full leafs with two half leafs and the right side had six full leafs. Hemi cars were not equipped with a rear stabilizer bar. The Hemi-powered Barracudas and Challengers all came with the heavy-duty Dana rear axle that rode on 15x7-inch wheels mounting F60X15 tires.

Motor Trend magazine writer Bill Sanders tested a new 1970 Hemi 'Cuda for the September 1969 issue. In his words, the new Hemi 'Cuda was "quite impressive." He wrote, "With the new Hemi 'Cuda a quarter-mile goes by so fast you hardly know you started. Even though our car had the widest optional F60X15 tires, we still experienced considerable wheel spin, which cut e.t.s. With a 4:10:1 axle ratio, all acceleration figures were out of sight, naturally. Plymouth's own version of the 'Shaker' hood adds to total performance." The Hemi 'Cuda Sanders drove was equipped with a TorqueFlite transmission, power steering, and power brakes, and it tripped the quarter-mile clocks in 13.7 seconds at a speed of 101.2 miles per hour.

Selling 666 units, the 1970 Hemi 'Cudas commanded the second-highest production numbers for any individual model Hemi-powered Chrysler product (the 1968 Road Runner is first). Of that total, 14 were convertibles. In 1970, 356 Hemi Challengers were produced; only

Bold colors were the norm for the early 1970s, and Plymouth pleased its customers with a long list of vivid colors that included Vitamin C, Lemon Twist, and this shade is called TorRed.

Nash Bridges' Hemi 'Cuda

Most of us remember Don Johnson as TV's "Miami Vice" detective who wore white suits over pastel-colored T-shirts, and drove a Ferrari. Today Don Johnson is still playing a cop, but he wears more-mainstream clothes while serving the city of San Francisco. He finally got wise and dumped the Ferrari for a real man's car—a 1971 Hemi 'Cuda. Well, that's what the movie folks would like you to believe. The car, or should I say cars (there are several), that Johnson drives are a taste of Hollywood movieland illusion.

How did Johnson decide on a 1971 Hemi 'Cuda? The story began when Don Johnson called movieland car czar Frank Bennetti into his production office. Bennetti has been supplying cars to the movie industry since 1980. Since then, Bennetti has supplied hundreds of cars to many television and movie projects. Johnson told Bennetti, "This is the car I've got to have." He showed him a photo of a Curious Yellow 1971 Hemi 'Cuda in a book. "The hair stood up on the back of my neck," Bennetti said. "I knew that was the hardest car to find." He explained to Johnson how few 1971 Hemi 'Cuda convertibles had been manufactured. It would cost a king's ransom to obtain one, much less several, for the upcoming television production schedule.

Bennetti offered look-alikes modified to suit their needs. A deal was struck for three 1971 Hemi 'Cuda convertible look-alikes. The Curious Yellow Hemi 'Cuda Johnson saw in the book had been photographed at sunset and took on a much more yellow/orange hue than the original Mopar Curious Yellow paint. As it turns out, Curious Yellow washes out to a pale yellow shade on movie film. All the cars had to be painted a brighter yellow in order to appear the correct color on film. A Sherwin-Williams industrial paint was selected, which Bennetti calls "school bus yellow." Other items demanded by Johnson's production company were a 1970 Parchment interior, working white convertible tops, and nondescript white letter tires on 14-inch Rallye wheels. And all of the cars had to work on the same ignition key.

On a very short schedule, Bennetti, with the help of Mopar restoration specialist Alan Foxx, completed the three cars. Two of the original cars started life as 1970 Barracudas. One of the cars is powered by a modified 360-ci engine backed by a four-speed trzansmission. This is Johnson's favorite car. The other two have 440-ci engines and automatic transmissions. One of the 440-powered cars is equipped with Flowmaster mufflers and it's used for all the show's engine sound recordings. The cars have all been modified with heavy-duty K-members, KYB shocks, heavy-duty torsion bars, and disc brakes.

All four of these cars are in a constant state of change, depending on the needs of the show's production crew. Recently, all of the interiors were replaced with correct 1971 Parchment interiors. Future plans call for safety drive-shaft loops to be installed on all four cars, along with the possibility of adding fuel cells to the three cars with standard tanks. Fiberglass replacements have been offered for the rare 'Cuda front-end sheet metal, but the production crew demands the real thing, even on the jump car. There has been talk of adding a real Hemi car to the group so open hood shots can be filmed.

When all four cars are together, it's nearly impossible to tell them apart. I guess that's part of the movie illusion we all love.

These look-alike 1971 Hemi 'Cudas make up the fleet for the "Nash Bridges" television series. From a few feet away, even the guys who built them can't tell one from the other. None of the cars has a Hemi under the hood.

In 1971, Billboard stripes replaced the hockey sticks. Throughout the era of the street Hemi, this was the most pronounced and extravagant display of engine size.

At a cost of close to $5,000, a new 1971 Hemi 'Cuda was not inexpensive in its day. Today, it would take almost 10 times that amount to buy one of the few produced.

nine were convertibles. The 1970 Challenger also accomplished its mission of outselling the Mercury Cougar. In total, the Challenger sold more than 76,000 units compared to the Cougar's 72,000.

For 1971, only minor but distinctive changes were made to the Barracudas and Challengers. The Barracuda's grille was restyled by adding four additional vertical bars. This new grille is commonly called a "cheese grater" by collectors because of its similarity to the kitchen appliance. The two large headlights were replaced with a quad headlight arrangement similar to the Challenger's. The grille was either painted argent silver or body color. Barracudas with chrome bumpers received the argent grille, and those equipped with the Elastomeric bumpers received a body color grille. Four nonfunctional louvers were added to the sides of the front fenders. These louvers are commonly called "gills" for obvious reasons. Thin chrome wheel opening moldings were added, and the taillights were slightly revised. If you had a high-performance engine in your 1971 'Cuda, why not advertise it to the world with Billboard stripes? These stripes replaced the hockey stick stripes. They were enormous, covering most of the quarter panel and half of the door. In foot-high letters on the leading edge, the billboard announced to the world the cubic-inch displacement of the high-performance V-8 under the hood or, in the case of the Hemi, displayed those four famous letters HEMI.

The 1971 Challenger grille also received a minor change. The full-width inset chrome rectangle was split in the center into two smaller rectangles. In the rear, the full-width taillight was split into two and the center backup light was integrated into the lens on each side. The

All 1971 Hemi 'Cudas came standard with F60x15 tires on 15x7 steel rims. Rallye rims, standard on all 1970 'Cudas, were optional in 1971.

R/T hardtop received a new set of wider body side stripes that terminated at the C-pillar. For 1971 the R/T convertible was discontinued.

Production numbers for both the Barracuda and Challenger declined drastically in 1971. The total production for the Barracuda and 'Cuda was only 16,159, compared to 50,627 in 1970. Hemi 'Cuda production for 1971 broke down to 108 hardtops and only seven convertibles. The Challenger's sales were down to just under 23,000 units. Of that number, only 71 were equipped with the Hemi engine.

4

Defining a Decade of Drag Racing

Hemi Drag Race Cars

In motor racing history, 1964 was a watershed year. The previous year, General Motors had pulled the plug on factory support of any type of racing, leaving Ford and Chrysler to battle in the heavyweight classes. Ford was refining the 427 for both drag racing and the oval tracks, and at Chrysler, the engineers reached back to a proven performer—the Hemi.

Development work on the new generation Hemi engine began in 1962 when a request was made to the Chrysler engineering staff to develop an engine suitable for both oval tracks and drag strips. The Hemi design was the obvious choice for many reasons. The positioning of the valve allows the intake charge flows straight into the chamber and straight out through the exhaust valve, which makes the design a natural choice. The combustion

The Plymouth and Dodge A-990s were Chrysler's front-line offense in the 1965 Super Stock battles. Bill Jenkins, driving a white Plymouth similar to this one, emerged victorious at the 1965 NHRA Winternationals.

83

The A-990's TorqueFlite transmission was modified for manual operation only. The shift pattern was reversed from that of a standard passenger car to prevent accidental shifting into reverse.

chamber's spherical design provides maximum volume with a minimum surface area. The spark plug is placed near the center of the combustion chamber for optimal fuel burn. The design of the cylinder head allows the use of large valves. The 1964 competition Hemi engine was similar only in basic design to the previous version last seen in 1958.

When the race Hemi first appeared in 1964, it was equipped with two Carter AFB carburetors. These were soon replaced with a pair of Holleys. The air horns on top of these Holley carburetors seal against a rubber boot on the bottom side of the hood's scoop opening.

The new blocks were extremely sturdy with cross-bolted main bearings.

The new Hemi made an auspicious debut at the 1964 Daytona 500 by taking the first three spots. Although the Hemi was introduced too late for the 1964 NHRA Winternationals, soon after many Hemi-powered Plymouths and Dodges were breaking track records across the nation. These specially prepared cars were available to the general public on a limited basis. Race teams with proven records in competition were the favored recipients.

The first 1964 Hemi cars built for drag racing were built in the lightest two-door sedan bodies available, the Plymouth Savoy and the Dodge 330. A liberal use of aluminum body panels and the crafty removal of unnecessary extras (rear seat, sun visors, arm rests, etc.) reduced the car's overall weight. The battery was placed on the right side of the trunk for increased traction and weight distribution. The new Hemi cars were easily identifiable by their large hood scoop and by the absence of the inboard upper beams from the standard quad headlights.

The Hemi engines that powered these drag cars were similar to the Hemi that powered the winner at Daytona. Instead of the single four-barrel carburetor dictated by NASCAR, drag racers were given multiple carbs. Chrysler engineers used the short cross-ram design from the successful max-wedge engines and adapted it to the Hemi. On top of the new aluminum manifold was a pair of Carter AFB carburetors. Only the early 1964 Hemi cars were equipped with the dual Carters. They were soon replaced with twin Holley carburetors. Two compression ratios were available: 11.0:1, which produced 415 horsepower, and 12.5:1, rated at 425 horsepower. Only two transmissions were available in 1964, a four-speed manual and the TorqueFlite, and it was the last year for the push-button shift.

At the two biggest drag racing events in the

When the Hemi-powered Dodges and Plymouths first appeared at the drag strip, each was equipped with a large hood scoop that had a rectangular opening. With no additional power accessories, the engine compartment of this former race car seems vast, even with the large Hemi engine in place.

The A-990s interior was merely functional. The seats were from a Dodge van and weighed only 22 pounds each. There was no insulation under the carpet, no radio, and no heater. The fire extinguisher and gauges have been added by the owner.

summer of 1964, the Hemi-powered Dodges of Roger Lindamood and the Ramchargers were dominant. The AHRA (American Hot Rod Association) held its Summernationals in Gary, Indiana, and there the Ramchargers were victorious against Lindamood. One week later at the NHRA Nationals in Indianapolis, Lindamood returned the favor, beating the Ramchargers with an elapsed time of 11.31 seconds and a speed of 127.84 miles per hour. Later at the Super Stock invitational in Cecil County, Maryland, a large fleet of Hemi-powered cars competed

against the factory Fords and Mercuries in a 30-car field. The rules were relaxed, allowing cars that normally competed in the Factory Experimental classes to run against Super Stock entries. Here, the Hemi cars were running elapsed times in the high 10-second range at 130 miles per hour. At the end of the night, the final run pitted Bud Faubel's Hemi Dodge against "Dyno" Don Nicholson's Comet. At the time, Nicholson was one of the best drivers and tuners around, and his Comet was running times comparable to the fastest Hemi cars. Nicholson won and

Hemi Clone Cars

It looks like a Hemi car. It sounds like a Hemi car. It runs like a Hemi car. It must be a Hemi car! Today, that's only partially true, since many of the Hemi-powered cars being driven are clone cars or replicas—a slick combination of the correct components and a few aftermarket pieces designed for the street.

A few years ago, clone cars were the scourge of the car collecting hobby. Unscrupulous car builders found that they could realize larger profits by installing a rare engine option in their restoration. Many made the conversions adroitly, fooling the experts. This easy money led to a tide of fake GTOs, big block Corvettes, and Hemi cars. Today, a clone car is an acceptable way for the enthusiast to get behind the wheel of the car of his dreams for a much lower price than the rare original. A case in point is Mel Wojtynek's A-990 clone.

Wojtynek loves big-block high-performance cars and he knew that the Hemi-powered 1965 Plymouth A-990 was one of the baddest of the breed. Wojtynek, who lives in southern California, also loves to drive his cars. A real A-990, in today's market, is worth approximately $80,000. That kind of value plus an engine with 12.5:1 compression takes all the fun out of a daily driver. Wojtynek contacted Bob Mosher, at Mosher's Musclecars. Mosher restores and builds replicas of 1962 through 1965 Mopars. He has two "factory demo" clones in the form of a black 1964 Max Wedge Plymouth Savoy and a Hemi-powered 1965 Belvedere A-990. One ride in Mosher's 1965 Hemi car and Wojtynek was convinced: He ordered a 1965 A-990 Hemi.

The cars Bob Mosher builds are works of art. They faithfully hold to the look of the originals with certain allowances for current technology. Wojtynek wanted a more powerful engine and had a 526-ci stroker engine built. The crankshaft is a Keith Black billet steel with a 5/8 stroke. A special Crower roller cam was ground. The heads are Stage V aluminum with 10.5:1 pistons. Backing an engine estimated to develop 700 horsepower is a heavy-duty TorqueFlite transmission and a 3:73 Dana rear end.

Wojtynek took his A-990 look-alike—with just 175 miles on the odometer—to Carlsbad Raceway in Carlsbad, California. He opened the headers, spiked his tank that was full of pump gas with a few gallons of racing gas, and bolted on a set of slicks. Wojtynek did a short burnout to heat the slicks, staged, and when the tree counted down, he punched it. On his first pass he turned an 11.58 elapsed time and 119 miles per hour. Later that day he ran an 11.40 elapsed time and a speed of 120 miles per hour. One week later, Wojtynek drove his A-990 imitator from San Diego to Bakersfield for the NHRA Hot Rod Reunion. The big Hemi never missed a beat during the 400-mile round trip, while registering 10 miles to the gallon.

As a sidebar to this sidebar, I recently had a chance to drive Wojtynek's Hemi Plymouth. When I got out of that car my knees were weak and my hands were shaking. I've driven quite a few high-performance cars in my life, but never one with such throttle response. What a car!

As Mel Wojtynek drops the hammer on his 1965 Hemi, the rear tires instantly turn into embers. Wojtynek's 1965 Plymouth is not an original A-990, but a carefully crafted clone capable of 120-miles-per-hour drag strip passes and casual trips to the local cruise-in.

ironically took home a Hemi engine as part of the prize package.

In 1964, some of the competitors found that if they altered the wheelbase of their cars, they could get more traction and thereby quicker elapsed times. These chassis alterations took the form of moving the front and rear wheels forward, while keeping the engine in the same relative location within the body. This change redistributed more weight to the rear wheels. In 1965, the alterations became more radical, and cars with totally changed proportions were not unusual. Due to the rule structure, classes that allowed chassis modifications also allowed engine changes. Soon the Hemi's dual four-barrel carburetors and large hood scoop gave way to Hilborn fuel injection units with 14-inch-long tuned stacks.

While fun to watch in competition, these cars could not be bought at the local Dodge or Plymouth dealership. In some cases, they lost most of their product identity due to the radical changes that were implemented in the search for speed. But there would be a Hemi-powered alternative available in 1965—the A-990.

In the November 1964 issue of *Plymouth Views*, Chrysler Corporation's Lynch Road Assembly Plant employee newsletter, it was announced that the new 1965 Super Stock Plymouth Belvedere and Dodge Coronet had gone into production that month in an article entitled "Plymouth, Dodge Dragsters With 426 Engines Built Here." The article covered the features of the special cars, and the fact that they were being built to meet the specifications of the major drag racing sanctioning bodies. The photo accompanying the article showed a veteran Lynch Road employee looking under the hood of one of the new Belvederes.

These specially built Dodges and Plymouths, all two-door sedans, came to be known by their engineering code—A-990. The A-990s were understated and audacious and built strictly for drag racing. For

Dick Landy made a career out of racing Hemi-powered Dodges. In 1968, he teamed up with his brother Mike (on the right), who raced the Dodge R/T, for a two-car assault on the nation's drag strips. In addition to racing, the Landy brothers held performance clinics at Dodge dealerships. Dick Landy

1965, the NHRA dictated that cars designed for Super Stock competition could no longer substitute standard body panels with those of fiberglass or aluminum. In 1964, NHRA required Ford to remove the fiberglass front bumpers on the Thunderbolts. It was the NHRA's plan to stop the proliferation of exotic lightweight parts in the stock classes. In 1965, factory experimental classes allowed competitors to exercise their creativity in weight reduction. Chrysler's engineers came up with their plan to comply with the rules, but still lighten the car as much as possible. They removed everything from the car that was not required by federal or state law and made the exterior sheet metal as thin as possible. Special body panels were built that were approximately half the thickness of a standard steel panel. This sheet metal abatement plan also included bumpers. The windshield was the only piece of real glass. All other windows were acrylic and the door hinges were made of aluminum.

The body was devoid of any sound-deadening material or seam filler, and certain small body

For the 1968 drag racing season, Chrysler engineers were given the green light to develop the ultimate factory door slammer. Dodge Darts and Plymouth Barracudas were chosen as the starting point for development. These cars were thoroughly lightened, and the big Hemi engine was added.

splash shields were deleted. The only modification needed to fit the Hemi into the engine compartment was a rework of the passenger side shock tower. This modification was also performed on the 1964 Hemi cars. There was no external badge denoting the engine size. The only giveaway that this wasn't an ordinary sedan was the oversize hood scoop.

All A-990 cars had a tan vinyl interior; there were no other choices. In the front were a pair of small bucket seats from an A-100 van. These seats lacked adjusters and were mounted to the floor with lightened brackets. The carpets had no backing or insulation. The quarter windows were fixed in place

and there was no rear seat. A large piece of thin cardboard covered the area where the seat back should have been. The front door panels did not have even the smallest arm rest. They too were deleted in the interest of saving weight. The instrument panel had plates blocking off the opening where the radio and heater controls would have been on any standard Belvedere or Coronet. To even further reduce weight, the sun visors, coat hooks, and dome light were deleted, and only a driver side windshield wiper was installed.

The engine was the Race Hemi, which had proved itself so well in the drag races in 1964. Now

The Little Red Wagon (left) and the Hemi Under Glass were initially built for drag racing competition. Because the weight distribution was heavily biased toward the rear wheels, both cars were easily able to do crowd-thrilling wheelstands. Soon they became an attraction because they could carry the front wheels for the entire quartermile. Chrysler Historical/Bob Riggle collection

fitted with aluminum heads, it was only available with a 12.5:1 compression ratio. The intake manifold for the A-990s was the same basic design as the one used on the drag cars in 1964, except now the material of choice was magnesium.

Other than the exterior color, the only other option was the transmission. The buyer had the choice of a heavy-duty four-speed manual with a Hurst shifter or a TorqueFlite that had a modified valve body, requiring manual shifting. In 1965, Chrysler abandoned the push-button control of the automatic transmission for a more conventional column shift. To facilitate trouble-free shifting during a drag race, all TorqueFlite equipped A-990s had their shift pattern reversed. The lever would be moved down one detent for the one-two shift and then down again for the final shift into third.

The exhaust system on the A-990s was also unique. The tubular headers swept underneath into 3-inch collec-tors where 2 1/2-inch pipes joined together and ran rearward to a single muffler, which mounted transversely under the rear bumper. The reason for a full system was a new NHRA rule for 1965. But the muffler was located to concentrate as much weight as possible over the rear wheels. The exceptionally large battery was mounted in the trunk for the same reason. All of the A-990 cars came with a Sure Grip rear axle with 4:56 gears. The rear springs were heavy-duty and were configured to locate the rear axle 1 inch forward of the standard mounting location. This shortened the wheelbase on the Plymouth from 116 inches to 115 and on the Dodge from 117 inches to 116. Pulling the rear wheels forward changed the balance of the car, adding more weight on the rear wheels. These A-990 cars were eligible to run in the Super Stock class. At the 1965 NHRA Winternationals, the Super Stock field was composed entirely of A-990 Plymouths. Bill Jenkins, who ran an elapsed time of 11.39 seconds at a speed of 126.05 miles per hour

Mick Weise has been racing this Hemi Dart for over 30 years. Here at Bakersfield's Famoso Drag Strip, he lifts the left front wheel off the ground on hard acceleration. This car continually proves the unbeatable power of the Hemi by running elapsed times as low as 10.13 seconds at speeds as high as 139 miles per hour.

in the final run, came out on top. Fast and durable, many A-990s were rebuilt into altered wheelbase cars. The few that survived are stunning examples of mid-sixties Super Stock technology.

In the mid-1960s, a peculiar show evolved from the competition in the Super Stock and Factory Experimental cars classes. A few smart competitors came to realize that there were other ways to make money at the drag strip. They saw the reaction of the crowd when one of the cars would pull the wheels off the ground at the start. If the reaction was good for a small wheelie, it would probably be fantastic for a big wheelstand. Before long, two Hemi-powered wheelstanding cars—*The Little Red Wagon* and the *Hemi Under Glass*—were thrilling crowds across the country. What's really amazing is that both of these cars were initially designed to be competitive race cars—not wheelstanders.

The Little Red Wagon started life as a docile Dodge A-100 compact pickup truck. Dick Branster and Roger Lindamood—the brain trust of the Color Me Gone Super Stock—took over a project started by two fellow Detroiters, Jim Collier and Jim Schaeffer. The concept was simple—put a big Hemi engine in the back of a light pickup. A small sub-frame held the engine, transmission, and rear axle. The truck's front suspension was the stock beam axle.

The other famous wheelstander, the *Hemi Under Glass*, was also conceived of in Detroit at the Hurst Performance Products engineering lab. The goal was to build an exhibition car that would display Hurst components. A 1965 Barracuda was selected. Only major surgery would have allowed the big Hemi engine to be installed in the Barracuda's minuscule engine compartment. Therefore, it was installed in the rear, fitted into a sub-frame similar to *The Little Red Wagon*'s. Unlike *The Little Red Wagon*, the *Hemi Under Glass* was initially built with a four-speed manual transmission. What else would the premier builder of four-speed shift linkage install? Many of the components in the independent rear suspension were borrowed from the Corvette, as was the trunk-mounted aluminum radiator. In a fit of overkill, the Hurst engineers sent the front sheet metal out for an acid bath. They also replaced the large rear window with one fashioned of Plexiglas. It was designed to be easily removed to service the engine.

Because the short wheelbase placed most of the weight over the rear wheels, traction was phenomenal. From the starting line, both of these cars could snap the wheels off the ground and carry them clear through the traps. *The Little Red Wagon* and the *Hemi Under Glass* toured the nation, amazing drag racing fans with their aerial acts.

In 1967 Chrysler once again experimented with

lightweight cars for the drag strip, but rather than using a race Hemi, these cars were powered by a modified street Hemi. Special lightweight versions of the Plymouth GTX and Dodge R/T were assembled. These cars assaulted the Super Stock B class, with Mopar drivers Ronnie Sox and Dick Landy leading the charge. Documentation confirms that 55 Dodges and 55 Plymouths were made, all of them white with black interiors. To run as light as possible, the heater, hub caps, sway bar, body sealer, or sound deadener were deleted. Customers buying one of these special cars were required to sign an agreement acknowledging that the car was not warrantied.

In 1968, Chrysler again went all out for the Super Stock ranks with specially built Hemi-powered Darts and Barracudas. These cars were the invention of Chrysler's Dick Maxwell. Maxwell, a Chrysler engineer and Ramcharger Club member, felt that putting the powerful Hemi engine in the smaller A-body Darts and Barracudas would create unbeatable drag racing cars. Within Chrysler there was a considerable amount of discussion about whether these cars should be built or not. Getting the approval to produce these special drag-race-only vehicles was a tough sell to management. The current musclecar boom and Chrysler's dedication to racing contributed heavily to the project's approval.

Chrysler engineer Bob Tarrozi developed the specifications and built a prototype on a Barracuda platform. Because both the Barracuda and Dart were built on the same platform, the modifications made to shoehorn the big Hemi into the Barracuda would be identical for the Dart. Reworking of the front spring towers and the special brake master cylinder (necessary because of the width of the engine) were the two most difficult modifications. The balance of the modifications lightened the car.

Other than the large scoop on the hood, the only other visible modification made to the 1968 A-body race cars was the enlarged rear wheel openings. This was done to accommodate the large slicks necessary to get the Hemi's power to the ground.

The front fenders and hood, with its oversize scoop, were made of fiberglass. The body panels and bumpers were acid-dipped to reduce the thickness of the metal. The heater, radio, rear seat, all body insulation, and sound-deadening material were deleted to save as much weight as possible. The two lightweight bucket seats were added from a Dodge van. The windows were made from a lightweight polymer, and all the window mechanisms were removed. The door windows were raised and lowered with a strap.

Once the prototype was approved, Chrysler contracted with the Hurst Corporation to build 50 Dodge Darts and 50 Plymouth Barracudas in the initial production run. Later, it produced an additional 25 of each car. Some sources claim Hemi Dart production totaled 83. All of these cars were shipped to the dealers with primer covering the metal body panels and the fiberglass front clip components in unpainted gel coat. None of these

Mr. Norm's High-Performance Dealership

When buying a high-performance Dodge in the 1960s, there was only one place to go to get the car, the parts, and the service—Mr. Norm's Grand-Spaulding Dodge. In the 1960s, many Dodge dealers sold high-performance cars, but only one specialized in them—Mr. Norm.

In the late 1950s, Norm Kraus (a.k.a. Mr. Norm) and his brother Lenny had been running a successful used-car lot in the Chicago area. Their specialty was high-performance cars. They went out of their way to fill their lot with tri-power and four-speed-equipped cars. Their success in the used-car field attracted the notice of the Chrysler Corporation. When a Chrysler representative approached them in 1962 with an offer for a Dodge dealership franchise, the Kraus brothers were very interested. What sealed the deal was the exciting new Ramcharger engine and Chrysler's commitment to performance cars. Ground was soon broken on the corner of Grand and Spaulding for the Kraus brothers' new dealership—Grand-Spaulding Dodge. In the fall of 1962, when the first 1963 Dodge cars were being delivered, the showroom was not complete, and the cars were stored outside in a hastily built corral.

As soon as the small Grand-Spaulding Dodge showroom was completed, it was filled with musclecars. Lots adjoining the dealership were crammed with as many as 350 high-performance Dodges. Customers could usually find what they wanted in dealer stock. A majority of the salesmen were former customers hired by Kraus because of their knowledge and passion for high-performance Mopars. The same was true for the parts and service department staff. Kraus also created a Mr. Norm's Sport Club for his customers. Members received a monthly newsletter and a discount on parts and service. Because of the special performance packages and the gearheads working in the service department, the Grand-Spaulding Dodges were always the fastest Mopars in the city. The best benefit of membership was the new car discount. Club members paid only a low,

In the Midwest, Mr. Norm's Grand-Spaulding Dodge was the place to go for high-performance Dodges. The dealership not only sold and raced them, but it also offered an abundance of performance packages from mild to wild.

no-haggle $200 over invoice for a new car, a figure that other dealers wouldn't match. Sport Club members were also treated to large open-house parties held in the service department of the dealership. Entertainment was provided by a live band, and plenty of food and soft drinks were served. When buying a new high-performance Dodge, customers found that the Grand-Spaulding trade-ins were always better than those of any other dealer. Norm loved to see the used-car lot filled with GTOs, Mustangs, and Camaros—all converts to the Mopar camp.

Three-quarters of the cars delivered at Grand-Spaulding Dodge were high-performance cars. In 1969 Mr. Norm's sales figures were $8.6 million, and in 1970 he took in a whopping $9.1 million. He regularly advertised on Chicago's powerful WLS radio station, whose signal reached far and wide, attracting new customers. Norm even offered to fly (one way) new car customers in from anywhere. The farthest someone came in to buy one of his cars was from Alaska.

When the insurance industry and government regulations killed the musclecar magic in 1971, Mr. Norm quickly shifted gears to van conversions. He offered the van customers the same level of customer service and value as his former high-performance clientele. Norm Kraus has retired from the car business, but hasn't lost his passion for the performance Dodges of the 1960s and 1970s. Today, Mr. Norm can be found at automotive events across the country, signing autographs and reminiscing about the halcyon days of Grand-Spaulding Dodge.

Between 1964 and 1971 there were two different shades of Hemi Orange. The race engines, like this one, were a slightly brighter shade. When the street Hemis were released in 1966, the engine color was changed to a more red-orange hue. This shade was used on all the street Hemis through 1971 and is the one commonly known as "Hemi Orange."

cars met the federal emission laws, and they could not be legally licensed for the street.

Chrysler's famous race Hemi engine, which featured 12.5:1 pistons, dual Holley carburetors on a magnesium cross-ram intake manifold, an aluminum water pump, and Hooker exhaust headers powered these purpose-built drag cars. The Hemi Darts and Hemi Barracudas were built with either a TorqueFlite automatic or a four-speed manual transmission. These specially built Barracudas and Darts were the last purpose-built drag racing cars to come out of Chrysler. Many of these cars have survived and are still racing today because of the excellent overall package and the powerful Hemi engine.

Hemi musclecars continue to do battle on the drag strips, nearly 30 years after their creation. In addition to regular competition on the NHRA Super Stock circuit, many Hemi owners enjoy a little grudge racing at a local track. Every year since 1995, the Pure Stock Musclecar Drags have been held at the Mid-Michigan Motorplex in Stanton, Michigan. The cars participating are limited to

The race Hemi engine was shoehorned into the small Dart and Barracuda chassis. One of the modifications that was necessary for engine clearance was a special master cylinder mount.

Each year a few hearty souls bring their Hemi cars to the Pure Stock Musclecar Drag Race. Anatol Vasiliev in his 1971 Hemi 'Cuda turned consistent 13.7-second quarter-mile elapsed times.

musclecars built between 1961 and 1974, and the cars must carry the factory-correct components for their year of manufacture. This precludes the use of headers, special ignitions, and slicks. This event is designed to put cars on the track that are representative of a well-tuned showroom stock musclecar—the kind of car you might face off against at a stoplight.

As you can imagine, the competition is hot and heavy, with a respectable showing from all musclecar manufacturers. Reigning as some of the fastest cars on the track are the Hemi-powered Mopars. Each year a few courageous owners bring out their elephant-engined cars to compete. With stock tires and tons of torque, getting a good bite off the starting line is the biggest challenge. Too much throttle can turn the rear tires into a barbecue in a matter of seconds. With a light touch, the driver of a Hemi car can get a respectable start with stock belted tires. Once the tires have taken a set, the throttle can be eased down. Upshifts can also break the tires loose, even with a TorqueFlite. It's a balancing act all the way down the strip.

In 1998, two Hemi 'Cudas ran at the event. Both of these cars were equipped with a Torque-Flite and 4:10 gears. They both ran consistently in the high 13-second range with speeds as high as 105 miles per hour. Hats off to the brave Hemi owners who won the admiration of musclecar enthusiasts for wringing out one of the baddest musclecars of all time.

Appendix

Street Hemi Specs

Type	90° OHV V8
Engine code	H, 1966; J 1967–1969; R, 1970–1971
Block	Cast iron with cross-bolted mains
Heads	Cast iron
Combustion chamber volume	168 cc min/174 cc max
Bore x stroke	4.25x3.75
Displacement	426 cubic inches
Horsepower	425@ 5,000 rpm
Torque (foot/pounds)	490@ 4,000 rpm
Compression ratio	10.25:1
Crankshaft	Forged steel
Pistons	Forged aluminum
Connecting rods	Forged steel
Intake manifold	Dual plane, cast aluminum
Carburetors	Dual Carter AFB (AFB-4139S front, AFB-4140S rear)
Camshaft	Mechanical (1966–1969) hydraulic (1970–1971)
Duration	276° (1966–1967) 284° (1968–1971)
Valve diameter	2.25 intake, 1.94 exhaust
Ignition	Dual point distributor with vacuum advance
Spark plugs	N-10Y Champion
Firing order	1-8-4-3-6-5-7-2
Exhaust	Cast-iron manifolds, 2.5 outlet

Index